THC MEDICINAL CANNABIS OIL EXTRACTION (RSO)

Strains, Methods, Uses, Dosage and Application

By William Bentley

INTRODUCTION:

In this book I'm calling the "Oil"; **THC** medicinal cannabis oil. It is commonly known as *Rick Simpson* Oil **(RSO).** Im not the inventor of this oil or the method of extraction, I'm just creating accessibility to the knowledge and how to apply it to your ailments in a safe and controlled environment.

The reason behind putting this literature together was because my own mother has struggled and battled with Lyme's disease for many years now, and through watching her suffer from many side effects of the disease (As well as the medication prescribed to her), I have compiled this book with all the information I can to make a bullet proof method of extracting the *medicinal oil* to treat herself safely in her own home.

Even if your a beginner and have never done this before this step by step guide should help you through your first oil extraction. Ive tried to answer the questions my mother was asking when medicinal cannabis oil was suggested to her numerous times, without going too deep into science. She just wanted the oil, and know how to make it safely to a high quality, she didn't want a science degree.

We are all lead to believe by the government that Cannabis is harmful, illegal and bad for you. Some people think all illegal drugs are bad and are of the same level of severity. Ive met people who are wrapped up in the propaganda that they think cannabis is on the same level as heroin, and it is not true. If you think this then you have been lied to, or had knowledge and education on drugs held from you. You must be reading this now out of the curiosity of its medicinal properties, or questioning what we have been told is good or bad for you.

I hope this helps you with your ailments the way it has helped my mother with hers.

THC & CBD (Cannabinoids);
How they work and what they mean:

It is understood that throughout the human body we naturally contain cannabinoid receptors, which are a part of the "Endocannabinoid system". This system is involved in various physiological processes such as pain sensation, appetite, memory and mood.

We know Cannabis, Hemp and Marijuana naturally possess different varieties of cannabinoids (Around 113). The most popular two been spoken about are;
THC (Tetrahydrocannabinol) and **CBD**.

One is very much legal (**CBD**) as it is extracted from hemp, and the other (**THC**) is illegal as it is extracted from various strains of cannabis/marijuana.

CBD oil is available in most holistic medicine shops on the high street. This book will be concentrating on **THC** oil. This is the oil you will have read about online or in the press, along with a string off success stories for been a miracle drug that is strangely illegal. **THC** is the medicinal oil that is known to shrink cancers into remission, help Alzheimer's and Parkinson's etc.

Is Cannabis Oil for me?

You have probably bought this book due to literature you have read online or seen in the press or on television. It has been a debate for years that the law and pharmaceutical industry have tried to shutdown from day one for the fear of loosing billions of pounds.

Imagine a natural plant that has grown on this earth for longer than we can even document, that has healing and medicinal abilities for many ailments and that can easily be grown at home. It would put the billion dollar pharmaceutical industries who are preying on the sick out of business. There is chemotherapy, radiation, chemicals and tablets with side effects that seem to need other tablets to heal and disguise those side effect. Im not berating the medicines out there but why not give cannabis oil a go? Regarding health you have nothing to lose to try it. It is either not for you, doesn't cure OR does cure. There is no negative damaging side effect or ailments to taking the Oil.

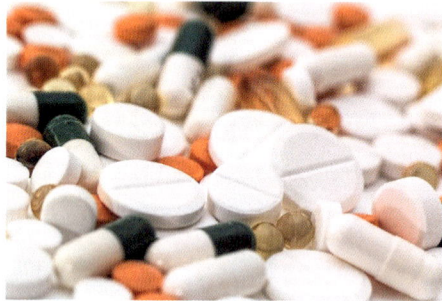

Im not saying Cannabis oil is a cure or your saviour, BUT if I was not getting the results I wanted from the medication prescribed or they were making me more sick I certainly for one would be considering giving this a try. The miraculous claims and hundreds of success stories are enough for me to want to try.

I would certainly not want to buy it on the black market either, for fear of been set up, caught, or for the fact there is no parameters put in place to ensure the oil I was buying is safely made and not cut, stretched or watered down to a lesser strain than required for maximum profit. I would want to make it myself to ensure the highest quality, and to ensure the best results for my body, mind and wallet. What ever you are charged on the street, there is a profit margin. Other wise they would not be selling it. Stay safe, make it yourself, and make it properly to a high grade as required in a safe environment.

Is there any side effects?

You are essentially digesting concentrated marijuana, so the side effects will be the same of consuming cannabis and can take up to a month to build up a tolerance to the effects.
You undoubtedly feel high, drowsy and sleepy, but please don't fight it as when your ill, poorly or sick the best remedy is rest, and your body recuperates when you sleep. You will acquire and gain a new larger appetite as the oil will effect your metabolism. Use this to your advantage and feed on healthy food that your body needs. Once again when you are ill or sick, your body needs nutrients and food for it to help repair itself. You will also experience dry mouth also known as cotton mouth. There is no harm in drinking water and staying hydrated. It can also help work towards a care free positive attitude which is always great if an illness is weighing on your mind. If anything the side effects of this oil are promoting eating, staying hydrated and helping you rest with ease. Generally just what a poorly person is always prescribed.
Until you build up a tolerance to these effects they may seem ten fold in the beginning. So be very careful if you operate machinery or drive. I wouldn't recommend it in the beginning until you are comfortable with the effects you are experiencing.

Is it 100% Natural?

Cannabis and Marijuana is a plant that over time has been enhanced by breeding and cross pollinating different strains to create stronger and larger yielding plants. In turn the plants have got more and more potent and stronger with a higher THC content. It is the THC that posses the effects that make us high. The cannabis today is not the same as the cannabis you may of read about in the 1960's. Its stronger and more powerful, which is perfect for achieving the medicinal qualities we want when extracting this oil. It is a plant that is 100% natural.

Cannabis and Cancer:

It is believed to be natures cure for cancer with many stories explaining how cancers have shrunk and gone into remission and sometimes disappeared completely, as well as reducing and helping many other ailments such as; Alzheimers, Parkinson's disease, multiple sclerosis, Crohn's disease, arthritis, HIV/AIDS, tumours, chronic pains, burns and much more.

Medicinal Cannabis has the potential to fight against cancer cells and prevent them from growing and spreading. By doing so the cancer has also known to reduce size and even disappear over time. Its believed it can prevent blood vessels from growing on the cancer which feed the cancer the nutrients it needs to grow and spread.

Different Strains of Cannabis, which do I use and why?

There are many different strains of cannabis, going on google or having a nosey around Amsterdam is like stepping in a candy shop. There is so many names, flavours and strains. **DO NOT WORRY**. You do not need to be a cannabis sommelier to source what you need. All the strains, flavours and names all fall generally under two categories, or think of it as one spectrum:

One side of the spectrum is **SATIVA** and the other side is **INDICA**. All the strains will be on this spectrum some possessing a higher ratio of one than the other or 50/50 etc due to cross pollinating of different breeds and strains,

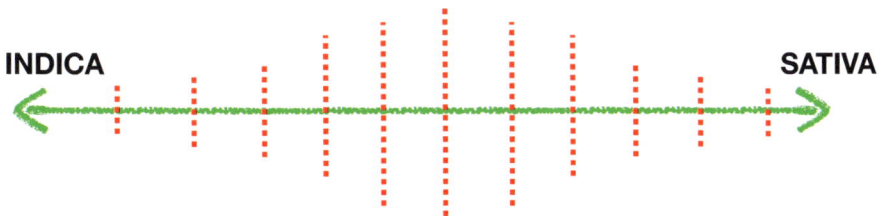

INDICA ←———————————————————→ SATIVA

INDICA strains generally posses a heavy stoned like effect providing a sense of deep body relaxation.
SATIVA strains provide a classic high with a more energising, lifting experience.
The Best Cannabis to use for our medicinal oil is that of the **INDICA** variety. **INDICA** heavy varieties offer a potent sedative medicinal property. Best results and the stories shared and read have all preached **INDICA** over **SATIVA.**

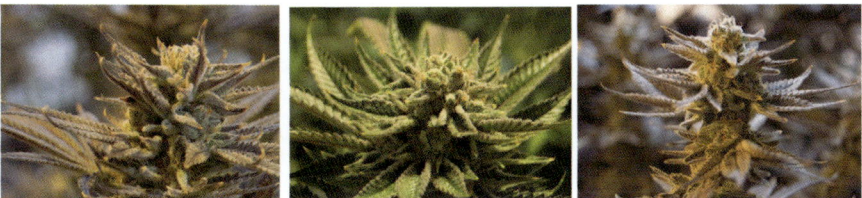

How much cannabis do I need?

To make the medicinal cannabis oil, you will need dried cannabis. The amount you need will all determine on how much oil you require, and the amount of oil you extract will depend on the strain and quality of your dried cannabis.

Typically **1 Ounce (28g)** of dried Cannabis will generally equate to **3g - 4g** of oil or **500g** of quality dried cannabis can do up to **60g** of Oil.

Though this will vary from strain to strain, its **THC** content and the quality of growth.

A pound of dried cannabis (**16 Ounces**) will equate to about **2 Ounces** of high quality oil

The quantity of cannabis is not as important as the quality. Low quality cannabis will still have the oil within it, but possess less. Higher quality cannabis will possess more oil, so the quality of the oil will be the same in the end after the extraction process because you are reducing it. The quality of the cannabis will determine the yield of oil as oppose to weight. *(So all the above weights consider as a ball park figure).*

How do I make Cannabis Oil?

Im writing this book so even if you are old and non technical, you can follow the instructions to create your own medicinal cannabis oil. The hardest bit will be to source your produce (*Cannabis*). I assure you that no matter how overwhelming it sounds it is not difficult or dangerous if you carefully follow these steps.

You will ned the following:

- **Cannabis (Desired amount)**
- **Solvent**
- **Rice cooker**
- **Large (untreated) wooden stirring stick**
- **2 x 20L plastic buckets**
- **stainless steel container**
- **clean container**
- **Large fan**
- **Oven mitts**
- **Coffee filter papers**
- **Water**
- **Plastic plunger syringes (No needles required)**

1. *Place your dried Cannabis into your plastic bucket*

2. *Douse enough to dampen the cannabis with the solvent you are using (Read Solvent chapter as to what solvent to use and why).* **2 Gallons (7.57 Litres)** *is required to extract the* **THC** *from* **1 pound (16 Ounces)** *of dried cannabis OR* **500ml** *is enough for* **1 Ounce (28g)** *of cannabis.*

3. *Using an untreated and clean piece of wood, Crush and mulch the cannabis in the Solvent until it is all broken up.*

Although the material is soaked and damp it will crush relatively easy as your cannabis is dry to begin with.

4. *Whilst crushing the material with your stick continue to add solvent until all your cannabis is completely covered and soaked. Continue to stir the mixture for **3 - 5 minutes**. Doing this will ensure that the **THC** and oils are dissolving off the plant and bonding to the solvent.*

5. *Steadily pour off the solvent/oil mixture into your second clean bucket. By now you have stripped the material of approximately **80% of its THC**. Don't throw away the contents of your first bucket!*

6. *Commence the second wash: Once again add more solvent to your original bucket or soaked damp cannabis and work for another **3 - 5 minutes** to extract the remaining **THC** and oils.*

7. *Pour off your solvent and **THC/Oil** mix again into the bucket containing your first mix that was previously poured off.*

8. *Discard and dispose carefully and wisely of your twice washed cannabis material.*

9. *Your bucket of the solvent oil mixture will now need filtering through a coffee filter paper into a clean container.*

10. *We are now going to use the Rice cooker as a devise to hold our desired temperature and boil off the solvent to separate the oil and solvent mixture. A rice cooker will boil it off nicely and hold over half a gallon of mixture. A rice cooker is designed to switch off at a certain temperature to stop your rice burning, this is the same temperature we require*

*for this process. **CAUTION:** you are boiling a very volatile liquid that is going to produce highly flammable vapours, keep away from stove tops, hot elements, cigarettes, sparks and naked flames, and of course in a well ventilated area. I would even suggest having a fan blowing gently to push away vapour etc. please stay smart, and please stay safe.*

11. *Add the solvent to the rice cooker until it is about **3/4 full** and turn on high heat (**COOK**). Continue to add your mixture to the cooker as solvent evaporates until you have added all your mixture to the cooker.*

12. *As your mixture reduces and decreases for the last time add a few drops of water (**A small soda cap full at most / about 10 drops of water for every pound of dry material used**). This is going to let the last bit of solvent release from the oil and bond the water whilst protecting your oil from too much heat. (**60g takes about half an hour to reduce so don't turn your back, and keep a keen eye throughout the process**).*

13. *When you are down to about one inch of solvent / water mixture in the rice cooker, place your oven mitts on and pick up the cooking unit and begin to gently swirl the mixture around the rice cooker and you will see the last bits of solvent boiling off.*

14. *Once the solvent is boiled off turn the cooker to low heat (**WARM**) and at no point should the oil ever reach above **290F or 140C**.*

15. *Using your oven mitts remove the rice pot from the cooking unit and gently pour the hot oil into your stainless steel container. You will undoubtedly have sticky oil stuck to the pan that will be difficult to remove. Feel free to use bread*

and mop up that oil, and eat the bread as a dose. But do be careful if your new and not as tolerant to the oil as it can take 30 minutes to an hour to feel the effects of what you have digested. So be careful not to take too much in the beginning.

16. *This next step has many options. Either Place this stainless steel container on a very gentle heating device (Dehydrator/ Coffee warmer/or carefully use a hairdryer) to dehydrate the oil. This is to remove the last bit of water and volatile turpentines that are left in the mixture. Commence until there is no more surface activity on the oil, then we can safely say the oil is ready for use. Another technique to finish the oil without the use of a coffee warmer or hair dryer, is to put the oil in a pre heated oven set at **120°C (250°F)** for thirty minutes to an hour, but be sure to keep an eye on your oil during this period as you do not want your oil to burn. Both of these methods work very well to bring the oil to a finished state.*

17. *Whilst the oil is warm, pliable and malleable, take your plastic plunger syringes and draw up the oil into the syringes. Once the oil completely cools it will have a thick glue/grease like consistency.*

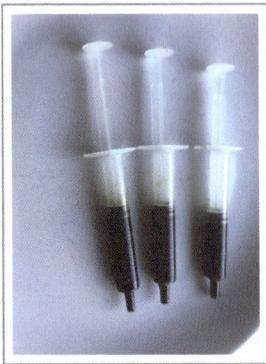

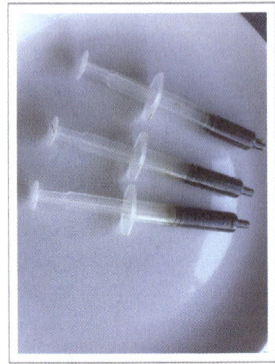

Why do we use a Solvent?

We use a solvent because the solvent is alcohol based and of a high ABV (Alcohol By Volume). The reason been is that alcohol is oil soluble and water soluble at the same time due to its chemical make up. This means we can use the solvent to bond with the oils within the plant and it is also strong enough due to its high alcohol content to rip through the plant matter and extract the oils we need. Once we have achieved this and taken the oil from the plant and removed the plant matter through basic filtering (Coffee Filter), then we are left with a murky brown liquid that we have to use our basic knowledge of distillation/separation/extraction to remove the alcohol from the oil. This sounds difficult but when we know how, it is quite easy. As the Alcohol and the oil both have a different boiling point we are going to exploit this with careful control of a heat source (Rice Cooker), so we can ride the temperature hot enough to evaporate the solvent (Alcohol) but not hot enough to burn or evaporate the oil. This is essentially distillation on a very basic level.

Which Solvents do I need to use and is it safe?

You want to be sourcing a clear solvent such as Ether, Naphtha or 99% Isopropyl alcohol. These solvents are strong enough to remove the oils and resins we need to make the medicinal oil.

Light Naphtha is not only cheap but available in most countries and very effective at doing the job. In some countries it is also known as Benzin(e) and is sometimes sold as cleaning fluid / Solvent at various hardware stores.

Remember any solvents you choose to use must be colourless like water. A good test is also to dip your finger in it and if in around 40 seconds it has evaporated leaving no oily residue behind, then this is the solvent for the job. If you are struggling in hardware shops please do try fuel suppliers etc. let them know you are looking for a solvent that reaches boiling point around 70C. It is sometimes used to fuel stove camps and lamps, degreasing engines or thinning paint. Just be sure to check it has not been mixed with anything else for extra uses (like rust inhibitor etc).

Why Do we add Water at the end?

A small amount of water is added near the end of our distillation / separation for the last amount of solvent to bond to the water (As I mentioned earlier that alcohol is water and oil soluble, but remember that water is not oil soluble), so then we can be sure to remove the solvent 100% from our oil without our oil beginning to burn as the last bit of solvent will have bonded to the water. Then next step is to gently keep the oil warm to reduce the oil by evaporating the little measure of water that we added. This is very similar to reducing a stock or a gravy, we are essentially removing the water to let the remaining ingredients thicken; IE the oil. (Basic Reduction). This will also take the oil to a medicinal strength. This reducing technique is called decarboxylation.

What do I do with the finished product?

Now you are left with a dark brown sticky glue like substance (Resin/Oil) in the bottom of your Cooking vessel (Rice Cooker). As it cools down it will slightly harden and become less pliable and malleable, so lets take advantage whilst its still warm. I find the best way to remove the oil is using a plastic syringe (Without the needle) and whilst the oil is still warm suck it up into the syringe. This is also perfect for keeping the oil and dispensing measured doses when required. As most syringes have measurements on the side it is also a great way to work out and calculate your final yield so you can then in turn work out your dosages and how long your yield is going to last before making more if required.

Storage?

It is recommended to store in a cool dark environment such as a refrigerator.

Different doses and duration of use?

The following is not medical advice:
You can use the oil for as long as your medical condition exists. When you are feeling better and test results show it you can still continue to take the medicinal oil but at a reduced dose which is classed as a maintenance dose (**1g-2g Monthly**).

It can take the average person **90 days** to ingest a **60g** oil treatment. It is suggested people start with a dose **3 times daily** (*About the size of a half grain of Short grained uncooked rice*). You should take this dose every **8 hours** (*In the morning, in the afternoon and an hour before bed*).

Remember after ingesting you generally wont feel any effects until about an hour afterwards. So please do be aware fo this and don't take more, thinking it is not working.

A beginners dose would be equal to about **1/4** of a drop. After 4 days at this dosage which will be taken 3 times a day you then will be able to increase your dosage by doubling the amount every four days.

Following this dosage many people have claimed that they had not experienced the high sensation commonly known with cannabis. Remember none of us are the same and each will respond differently to it due to our tolerances (*Just like peoples tolerance to alcohol etc*). Which means some people will be able to raise their dosage a lot quicker than others. If you do feel a "High" sensation do not panic as it will not harm you in any way. Just learn to enjoy it. It can be very mellow and calming.

It can take **3 - 5 weeks** to get your tolerance built up so you can ingest **1g per day**. Once you reach this dosage you can continue at this level until your medicinal issues are brought under control. Once your tolerance has built up and you become used to the oil, each dose you are ingesting will equal to **8 - 9 drops every 8 hours**. Some patients have no problems ingesting more. It takes a dose equivalent to the size of **2 grains of rice** (*Short grain*) to equal **1 drop**. Once you are totally tolerant to the oils effects you are actually ingesting a dosage which is equal to **16 - 18 grains** of rice.

I have read about some cases online where patients have eaten the full **60g** Dosage in 1 month and as a result of it they have been declared cancer free. BUT, by using the slower dosage mentioned previously it allows time for your body to build up a tolerance to the oil, without you been put off (*If your new to the feeling of been high on cannabis*) and this will ensure a pleasure or enjoyment from the effects, and enjoy taking it.

Everybody is different and we all have a different tolerance to medication. But with medicinal oil even children can tackle the same doses with no detrimental effects.

Some people love the taste of this oil, but I understand it is not for everyone. If it is not your taste feel free to try eat it with bread or a piece of cracker to help the medicine go down.

BE CAREFUL TAKING THIS OIL ALONG SIDE OTHER MEDICATION OR DRUGS!
Please seek medical advise from a doctor who supports the use of medicinal cannabis oil if you are unsure, and ask about the use of this oil along side pharmaceutical medication.

MEDICINAL CANNABIS OIL WILL LOWER YOUR BLOOD PRESSURE!
If you are taking medication to lower your blood pressure it is very likely you will no longer require it. When taken alongside it, be aware that combined it can bring your blood pressure down to an uncomfortable level, and if you are unsure then check your blood pressure often in the beginning stages until you are comfortable with the dosages, the feeling and the effect it has on your body.

Alternatively if you suffer from low blood pressure you will need to find the right balance between your medication and the medicinal oil. Please always try to stay hydrated.

If you suffer from **diabetes,** you may find your need for insulin will be reduced and may even eradicate your need to use insulin or other pharmaceuticals. Whether it is type 1 or type 2 diabetes it is beneficial either way to use the oil and decrease the need for insulin whilst protecting your body from any other harm as a result from the disease.

When this medicinal oil is used along side morphine, painkillers and steroids it can cause terrible side effects. Some people reduce their prescribed medication by half on day one, then over the next week or two they will continue to reduce until stopped.

If it is cancer you are treating and this medicinal oil cannot reverse the cancer, it is not unusual for the patient to live many months more than recommended, and can experience a good quality life within this duration.

Damaged by Chemotherapy or Radiation?

People who are left damaged from Chemotherapy or Radiation can also look towards self treatment with medicinal oil. It is suggested to ingest **180g/180ml** of high quality cannabis oil, as quickly as they can and this will give a better chance of survival. This sounds a lot, but the extra **120g/120m**l suggested is to try reverse the damage received from the Chemotherapy and Radiation. It sounds a high dose but once the patient has become used to the medicinal oil, there should be no problems ingesting this amount in up to **5 - 6** months.

Treating Skin Cancers and Skin ailments:

Applying this medicinal oil direct to the skin usually only takes a few grams to accomplish the task. *(It should be noted when applying to skin or treating skin that medicinal oils produced from Sativa strains are just as effective as when in contact with the skin the patient will not feel or experience the high effect).*

Once applied to the troublesome area proceed to cover with a bandage. Remember to apply fresh medicinal oil and bandages every **3 - 4 days**. When no trace of the cancer is left, do still continue to treat the area for a further **2 weeks** to ensure all remnants of cancer cells are dead. If the cancer is well established before you start your treatment it could obviously take longer to see the desired effects. It could take ups to **3 weeks** upwards, it is all depending on how deep the cancer is embedded.

This method also applies to healing 3rd degree burns to prevent scarring. Or to help treat new scars.

Maintenance Dose:

Once you have put your ailment into remittance and ended your treatment, it is not foreign for many people to carry on taking the oil but at a much reduced "**Maintenance Dose**" to keep unforeseeable ailments at bay. Around **1g - 2g a month** would be a recommended maintenance dose. Just a little bit before bed will help with maintaining good health.

How to ingest?

You can place your dose under your tongue or up on your gums but personally if your not fan of the taste or worried of wasting it then there is no problem with swallowing the dose straight away, Sticking it under the tongue or on the gums would only be super beneficial if your problems or ailments were diagnosed in them areas.
Its pretty easy to stick the oil on your finger and scrape off onto your teeth and drink water, which you will swill around until it unsticks from your tooth, then swallow.

As mentioned before, bread or a cracker is a great way to disguise the taste or flavour, and easier to swallow if your not used to this process.

Suppository?

If you ailment is in the prostate or bowel region then using as a suppository is a fantastic idea to reach the problem area. But remember this way will enter the blood stream, bypassing your liver. So if it is the liver you are looking to treat please resort back to orally. You need to be clever and think; Where your ailments are and how is the best way you can get this oil into your system for that particular ailment.

If it is a life threatening disease such as cancer, when people stay within their comfort zone it is safe and good to see, but the honest truth is that the faster you take the oil and get it into your system, the better your chance of survival.

Epilogue:

I do hope this is enough information to get you on your way to safely make your own medicinal oil **(RSO)**, and to help treat your sickness and ailments. In desperate times people take desperate measures so please don't cut corners, be safe, sensible and if unsure seek further advice.

I wish you all the best

William Bentley

20871429R00015

Printed in Great Britain
by Amazon